JAN   2007

Predatory Drugs

Elizabeth Russell Connelly

Enslow Publishers, Inc.
40 Industrial Road
Box 398
Berkeley Heights, NJ 07922
USA

http://www.enslow.com

Library of Congress Cataloging-in-Publication Data

Connelly, Elizabeth Russell.
    Predatory drugs=Busted! / Elizabeth Russell Connelly.
       p. cm. — (Busted!)
    Includes bibliographical references and index.
    ISBN 0-7660-2474-1
    1. Drug abuse—Juvenile literature. 2. Drugs of abuse—Juvenile literature. 3. Date rape drugs—Juvenile literature. 4. Designer drugs—Juvenile literature. 5. Youth—Drug use—Juvenile literature. I. Title. II. Series.
    HV5809.5.N66 2006
    613.8—dc22

                                                                    2005029374

Printed in the United States of America

10 9 8 7 6 5 4 3 2 1

To Our Readers:
We have done our best to make sure all Internet Addresses in this book were active and appropriate when we went to press. However, the author and the publisher have no control over and assume no liability for the material available on those Internet sites or on other Web sites they may link to. Any comments or suggestions can be sent by e-mail to comments@enslow.com or to the address on the back cover.

Illustration Credits: BananaStock, pp. 40–41, 68; Courtesy of www.dea.gov, pp. 22, 32, 48, 63; © 2006 JupiterImages, pp. 4–5, 12–13, 17, 24–25, 27, 35, 50, 52–53, 78, 84; stockbyte, pp. 70–71.

Cover Illustration: Associated Press.

CONTENTS

CHAPTER ONE

PREDATORY DRUGS

Samantha and Melanie, both high school freshmen, were watching a video with a few friends.[1] One of the older boys gave Samantha a soda. It tasted different to her, so she asked Melanie to try it. Melanie agreed and gave it back to her. Samantha gulped it down anyway, and, within a few minutes, passed out on the couch. Melanie sipped her drink and rapidly felt drunk. She felt her body go numb.

When Melanie began vomiting, her friends carried her into the bathroom and laid her on her side so she would not choke. It was about 2:00 A.M. Still passed out on the couch, Samantha started gagging and throwing up in her sleep. Her friends carried her into the bathroom and laid her down next to Melanie.

About 4:30 A.M., they finally drove Samantha and Melanie to the hospital. One friend saw white stuff stuck in Samantha's throat and tried to clear it out. By the time they arrived, neither girl was breathing. Neither had a heartbeat.

For the next few hours, the girls looked the same in their stark white hospital gowns. Their eyes were shut and they had tubes stuck up their noses and down their throats. Melanie was breathing slowly and was put on a respirator. Unlike Samantha, vomit had not reached her lungs. The doctors said that if Melanie had gotten to the hospital a few minutes later, she would have stopped breathing, had a heart attack, and died. They said that Samantha was in such severe shock when she arrived at the hospital that she was essentially dead.[2]

By that evening, Samantha's heart had stopped beating twice, and it was becoming harder to revive. Her kidneys and liver had shut down. Her blood pressure kept dropping and her heart was working overtime trying to compensate for the failed organs.

Melanie came out of her coma late that afternoon, about seventeen hours after she had passed out on the bathroom floor. She gagged from the tube that went down her throat and into her lungs to help her breathe. Her arms were strapped to the bed. She was able to scribble questions on a piece of paper: What happened? Where's Sammy? Doctors rolled her bed over to the window of Samantha's room. Tears rolled down Melanie's cheeks.[3]

Samantha died two hours later.

Early the next morning, police searched the apartment where the girls had been drugged. They questioned the four males involved (ages 18, 19, and 26) and seized bottles and glasses, which were tested for drugs. Lab analysis showed that three glasses and seven beer bottles contained residue of GHB.

All four were arrested and faced manslaughter charges. Their trial began a year after Samantha's death. This was one of the first trials of a GHB-related death. The three younger males were found guilty of involuntary manslaughter and lesser charges of poisoning.[4] Two were sentenced to about five to fifteen years, and one got seven to fifteen years. The twenty-six year old was convicted of being an accessory to manslaughter, poisoning, and possession of marijuana and GHB. He received a three-to five-year sentence.

GHB

In 2002, the Drug Abuse Warning Network (DAWN), which tracks emergency department visits related to recent drug use, reported GHB to be second only to ecstasy as the club drug cited most often in emergency department admissions.[5] Emergency treatment for GHB jumped from 56 hospital visits in 1994 to 3,330 in 2002. Twelve to twenty-five year olds accounted for 56 percent of the GHB users admitted to emergency departments in 2002.[6] According to the U.S. Drug Enforcement Administration

(DEA), since 1990 GHB has been to blame for more than 15,600 overdoses and run-ins with the law. In the same period, GHB has led to at least 72 deaths.[7] The actual number of overdoses and deaths is even greater, but GHB leaves the body so quickly (from four to twelve hours after ingestion) that tests and autopsies do not always detect it. In cases where GHB was used in rape, the victims might not realize they were drugged and assaulted until the GHB has already left their system. No national statistics capture the number of sexual assaults involving GHB or Rohypnol.

Rohypnol

Reliable statistics on overdoses and deaths involving Rohypnol are difficult to measure for reasons similar to GHB.[8] Rohypnol may stay

MYTH		FACT
On GHB, even if you pass out, you will wake up fine a few hours later.	vs.	Too many people never woke up. Thousands who did, woke up several hours later in the hospital emergency department.

longer in the body than GHB—up to twenty-four hours in the blood, and up to four days in urine—but the amount may be too small to detect.[9] If someone were given it unknowingly, he or she may not recover from the drugging and get to the hospital before the Rohypnol is out of his or her system. Also, if unaware that Rohypnol was given, the hospital might not know to test for it. Most overdoses and deaths involving Rohypnol are the result of mixing it with other drugs—like cocaine, marijuana, and alcohol.[10] DAWN has not cited Rohypnol in recent reports, because the estimates they receive from hospitals have been too imprecise to publish.[11]

MYTH		FACT
If someone slipped a "roofie" into my drink, I would taste it.	VS.	Rohypnol dissolved in water might taste a little salty, but it is virtually tasteless in sodas, beer, and other drinks.

Ketamine

According to DAWN, in 2002 ketamine contributed to at least 260 cases that landed someone in the emergency department.[12] And those are only the cases where the person admitted to using ketamine; there are even more who never made it to the hospital.[13] In 2002, twelve to twenty-five year olds accounted for 68 percent of the ketamine users admitted to emergency departments in the United States.[14]

Opium dens were popular
in the late 1800s.

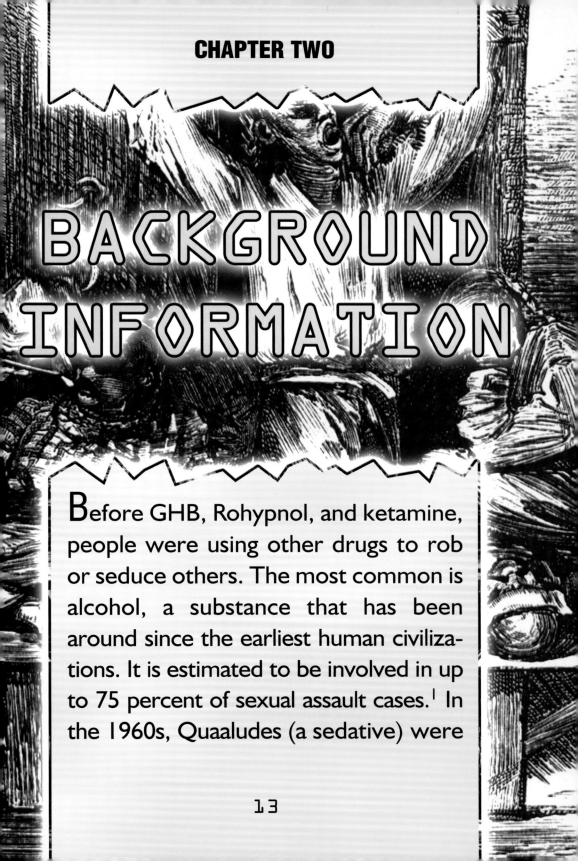

CHAPTER TWO

BACKGROUND INFORMATION

Before GHB, Rohypnol, and ketamine, people were using other drugs to rob or seduce others. The most common is alcohol, a substance that has been around since the earliest human civilizations. It is estimated to be involved in up to 75 percent of sexual assault cases.[1] In the 1960s, Quaaludes (a sedative) were popularly associated with lowering inhibitions. Today, use of prescription medications—such as Valium and Xanax—are on the rise.[2]

According to Dr. Alex Stalcup, the medical director of a drug treatment center in California, "Any drug in the hands of a sophisticated predator can be used to render someone helpless, but downers are the most prominently used."[3] Alcohol, GHB, and Rohypnol are all downers, which are drugs that slow down the central nervous system. Someone can slip one of these drugs into a drink without the victim knowing, and coax him or her into doing something he or she might not otherwise do.

A Brief History of Drugs

Drug use has been part of human civilization for millenia. Marijuana was used as medicine almost five thousand years ago.[4] Opium cultivated from the juice of poppy plants dates back as far as 3400 B.C. in Mesopotamia (present-day Iraq).[5]

In more recent history, soldiers returning home from the Civil War (1861–1865) became addicted to the painkiller morphine. Hoping to provide something less addictive, the Bayer Company developed heroin in 1898.[6] It turned

Top 10 Reasons Not to Do Drugs

1. You might do something to endanger your life or someone else's.

2. You put yourself in a compromising position. Rape is a very real risk with GHB, Rohypnol, ketamine—and alcohol.

3. You may permanently damage your brain, slowing down your memory and ability to learn.

4. You may vomit and choke, which could kill you.

5. You can become addicted without even realizing it.

6. If addicted, trying to quit is incredibly difficult and painful.

7. People who sell drugs often mix one drug with another without telling you. The combination can kill.

8. You could accidentally overdose.

9. Getting addicted or arrested could ruin your dreams.

10. You may say or do things you later regret.

out to be worse. To fight an increasing drug abuse problem, the federal government passed the Harrison Act in 1914. This made the recreational use of narcotics illegal. In 1915, the Bureau of Internal Revenue was created to handle drug law enforcement.[7]

Around the same time, a nationwide movement started by the Anti-Saloon League was pushing to make alcohol illegal, too. In 1920, their efforts paid off with the Eighteenth Amendment to the Constitution, which initiated a period called Prohibition. People could not legally drink or sell alcohol during this time, but the illegal flow of bootleg alcohol flourished. In 1929, the Great Depression forced people to reconsider Prohibition. The making and distribution of alcohol could provide jobs, and the tax on alcohol sales would pump much-needed dollars back into the struggling economy. In 1933, the Twenty-first Amendment repealed the Eighteenth. Prohibition was over.[8]

In the 1940s and 1950s, cocaine and methamphetamine were becoming popular on the streets. Mexican opium made its way to New York, where it was refined into heroin and distributed to cities around the country. Addiction was becoming a problem as more and more people were using these drugs. To stem the abuse, the Boggs Act of 1951 was passed. It set fines and made prison time mandatory (from two to twenty years) for anyone caught selling illegal drugs. Five years later, the Narcotic Control Act of 1956 increased the fines and did away with probation

In 1920, after the Eighteenth Amendment was added to the Constitution, speakeasies and other illegal bars opened.

and parole. It also added the death penalty for anyone eighteen or older who sold heroin to someone under eighteen years old.[9] As smuggling illegal drugs into the United States became a greater problem, the U.S. Customs Service also took on drug enforcement responsibilities.[10]

Despite these tough laws, drug use and abuse skyrocketed in the 1960s. Young Americans were questioning conventional values and exploring alternative lifestyles—which included illegal drugs. The federal government responded by taking a tougher stance on fighting drugs. In 1966, the Bureau of Drug Abuse Control (BDAC) was created.[11]

The crackdown on the traditional flow of illegal drugs led to basement laboratories making copycat drugs. One such copycat was GHB. Prescription medicine made by pharmaceutical companies was also being used illegally at parties and clubs. Ecstasy, though first made in 1912 by the pharmaceutical company Merck, became popular in the underground drug scene of the 1980s.[12] Ketamine and Rohypnol were also part of this trend.

By the early 1970s, President Richard Nixon

and Congress were concerned about the lack of cooperation among all the agencies responsible for tracking the illegal flow of drugs. In 1973, to better fight what President Nixon called "an all-out global war on the drug menace," the Drug Enforcement Administration (DEA) was formed. The DEA is responsible for managing the government's drug control activities. It works with the FBI to gather better intelligence on drug trafficking organizations.[13]

The DEA enforces the Comprehensive Drug Abuse Prevention and Control Act of 1970. It is commonly called the Controlled Substances Act

MYTH FACT

A little bit of GHB will not kill me.

vs.

Would you bet your life on someone who failed chemistry? Drug dealers making GHB in their bathtub do not worry about precise measurements. You never know how much you are getting from batch to batch.

(CSA) and is used to cut down the sale of illegal drugs. Since the Harrison Act of 1914, there have been more than fifty laws enacted to control drug abuse.[14] The CSA consolidated most of those laws to better regulate the manufacturing and trafficking of narcotics and the chemicals used in their production. The CSA also made possession of illegal drugs a misdemeanor and selling or transferring them a felony. The act places illegal drugs into one of five schedules, based on the drug's potential for abuse or addiction, medicinal value, and harmfulness.[15]

GHB is listed under the most dangerous category, Schedule I, which means it carries an extremely high risk for abuse and addiction. Most Schedule I drugs have no accepted medical use in the United States, but a prescription form of GHB is used in treating a very rare sleep disorder.

Ketamine falls under Schedule III, because its abuse potential is somewhat lower than Schedule I and II drugs, and it has an accepted medical use. Because Rohypnol is perceived to have an even lower risk of abuse, but still can lead to physical or psychological dependence, it is listed under Schedule IV. However, the DEA is considering reclassifying Rohypnol as a Schedule I drug.[16] When new evidence shows that a substance is more dangerous than previously thought, the DEA may reschedule it.

GHB, Rohypnol, and Ketamine

Each of these drugs can affect people in different ways—from drunkenness to unconsciousness or even coma and death. Each person reacts differently—depending on weight, height, how much food was eaten, and other factors. All three drugs can cause amnesia.

Despite the danger, some teens and college students take these drugs voluntarily for what they think is fun. In 2004, fewer than 2 percent of middle and high school students across the country used GHB, Rohypnol, or ketamine.[17] In contrast, the same nationwide survey found that 77 percent of students have consumed alcohol by the end of high school; nearly half have done so by eighth grade.[18]

GHB, Rohypnol, and ketamine (along with ecstasy) are called club drugs because people buy and use them at dance clubs and raves. Trance parties and raves go on all night and often take place in the middle of the woods, in open fields,

Ecstasy is an illegal drug sometimes sold at raves and clubs. The effects raise body temperatures and can cause death.

or in abandoned warehouses. Many people do not use drugs at these events. But those who do are gambling with their life.[19]

"A lot of people have misconceptions about what really goes on at raves," says DEA Agent Richard Woodfork.[20] "We have seen parents actually drop their kids off for them." In reality, says Agent Woodfork, "it's more like a club-drug superstore in there."[21] Raves revolve around getting high. In clubs, the digital displays on the walls and the repetitive beats synchronized with lasers and lights are all meant to put people in a trance state. Raves that take place in the middle of nowhere may not have the high-tech shows, but the drugs are everywhere.

The DEA categorizes GHB, Rohypnol, and ketamine as predatory drugs because some people use them to take advantage of others. The terms "date-rape" and "acquaintance-rape" drugs stem from their use in sexual assault.[22] Though many other drugs are used at raves and in assault crimes, this book focuses on GHB, Rohypnol, and ketamine.

CHAPTER THREE

GHB

Caleb was thirsty, so he took a few chugs from a water bottle.[1] What the twenty-seven year old did not realize was that the liquid was not just water, but a strong batch of GHB mixed in water. His friend had left it on the coffee table. Even after he found out what it was, he was not too concerned about the amount he drank. Caleb was familiar with the drug from the raves he and his friends liked to go to. In fact, he sometimes performed as a disc jockey at raves. He was the person friends would go to for advice on which drugs to take safely and which not to mix.

When Caleb passed out, his friends assumed he would sleep deeply for a while, then wake up like normal. His roommate checked on him every so often to make sure he was positioned on his side—to prevent choking on vomit, if any—and still breathing. Each time she nudged him, he would start snoring. A few hours later, when his roommate checked, she discovered that Caleb was not breathing.[2] She called 911 and tried to resuscitate him with CPR. In the ambulance, they got a faint pulse, but it faded away. After efforts to revive him, Caleb died on the emergency room table.

History

GHB was originally developed in the early 1960s as a general anesthetic. But because its effects were unpredictable and it did not work very well to prevent pain, no products were developed for commercial use.[3] Underground chemists began experimenting with GHB recipes. Starting in the 1980s, health food stores began selling GHB, promoting it as a sleeping pill, natural anti-aging drug, and bodybuilding supplement.[4] Bodybuilders and athletes began mixing the powder with water and drinking it. They believed it would strip away fat and fuel muscle growth. Word got out that GHB made people feel intoxicated and more sensitive

GHB was once sold in health food stores as a bodybuilding supplement. The effects were deadly.

MYTH		FACT
I've heard club drugs are harmless.	vs.	GHB, Rohypnol, and ketamine can cause amnesia. Many users cannot describe what happened, because they simply do not remember what they felt or did while under the drug's influence.

to touch. People wanting a legal alternative to ecstasy were interested in GHB. It was even hyped as an aphrodisiac, which increases sexual desire. Teens began using it at large all-night raves and eventually at private house parties.[5]

By 1990, poison-control centers and emergency departments were getting lots of cases involving GHB. Kids were showing up unable to breathe clearly, collapsing into seizures, and vomiting uncontrollably. Some were slipping into comas. As a result, the United States Food and Drug Administration (FDA) began investigating the drug. Later that same year, the FDA declared the sale and manufacture of GHB to be illegal.[6] Despite more information about the risks, body-builders still use GHB. But now they have to buy it illegally at gyms and clubs.[7]

It became known as a date-rape drug, because the powder was being slipped into drinks and given to unsuspecting victims, usually young women. The victims would pass out and wake up hours later, not remembering what happened. Too often, they had been sexually assaulted. In a few cases, they never woke up.[8]

The death of Samantha and another teenage girl led to the "Hillory J. Farias and Samantha Reid Date-Rape Drug Prohibition Act of 2000." Though there was no evidence of either girl being sexually assaulted, their deaths brought attention to GHB—a drug already known to be used in date rape. President Clinton signed the legislation to make it illegal to possess GHB. Now it is a controlled substance, just like heroin, which means the making and selling of the drugs are closely regulated by the federal government. If caught with it, a person could spend a year in prison and pay a fine of one thousand dollars. If the person provides the drug to someone else, he or she could spend up to twenty years behind bars. And if someone dies or is seriously injured because he or she supplied the drug, he or she could get the death penalty.[9]

As of July 2002, the FDA approved Xyrem, a prescription form of GHB. It is used only to treat patients with a rare sleep disorder. It is the only legal form of GHB. To prevent theft, the FDA and

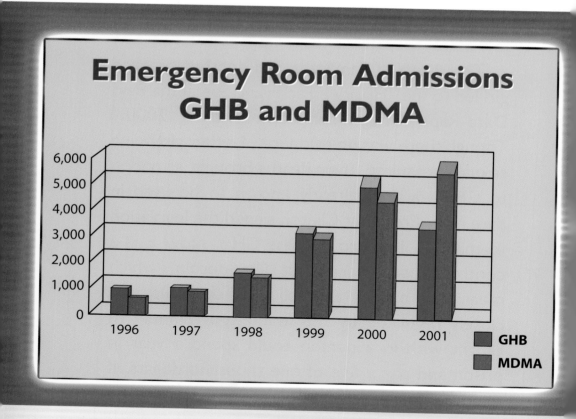

This chart shows how many people with GHB or MDMA (ecstasy) in their system during the years 1996–2001 were admitted to the emergency room.

drug manufacturer have put tight security around Xyrem. One centralized pharmacy distributes it to patients, only after they have been told about its proper use and the danger of abuse. Xyrem cannot be sold, distributed, or provided to anyone else.[10]

Also in 2002, a major DEA investigation called Operation Webslinger took down drug trafficking organizations that sold GHB, GBL, and BD over the Internet.[11] Operating out of several U.S. cities, the DEA worked with many other government agencies. U.S. Postal Inspectors and U.S. Customs tracked packages and shipments to and from the suspects. The IRS, the FBI, and Canadian law enforcement gathered intelligence. Agents ultimately arrested 175 people in the United States, Canada, and Europe.[12] The DEA estimates that the barrels they seized could have produced more than 25 million doses of GHB and its chemical cousins.

Chemical and Scientific Information

Called Liquid X on the street, GHB is short for gamma-hydroxybutyrate. It is made from solvents like fish-tank cleaner, floor stripper, and engine degreaser. The people who make it are called kitchen chemists, because they can easily make it in their kitchen sink or bathtub.[13] Sometimes, GHB is sold as a white powder, but usually it is a colorless liquid sold by the capful. It has almost no scent and might taste a little salty. But if diluted in a drink, a person probably would not taste the drug. GHB is illegal in the United States and Canada.

GHB has two commonly sold chemical cousins: gamma-butyrolactone (GBL) and 1,4 butanediol (BD). GBL and BD affect users in similar ways as GHB. The more law enforcement has cracked down on GHB, the more its cousins are being sold instead. Both are converted to GHB in

Operation Webslinger helped stop drug trafficking. The DEA seized GHB, and other drugs, that were sold over the Internet.

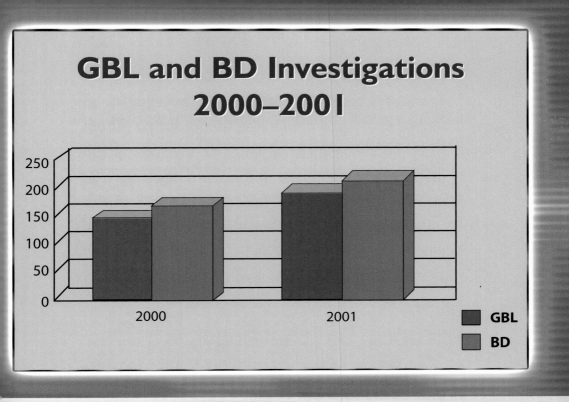

GBL and BD Investigations 2000–2001

250
200
150
100
50
0

2000   2001   ■ GBL
                            ■ BD

The DEA and other agencies investigated numerous cases of GBL and BD use.

the body. The body also produces tiny amounts of GHB, but scientists are not yet sure what its function is.[14] It occurs in small amounts in the brain, heart, hair, liver, and other organs.[15] This natural occurrence complicates testing, because it can be difficult to distinguish natural GHB from ingested GHB.[16]

Though some high school and college students take GHB voluntarily as a cheap way to feel drunk, it is also used against unwilling victims in sexual assault. Since it is rapidly absorbed and broken down by the body, GHB is hard to detect in tests. After swallowing it, the drug may stay in a person's blood for four to eight hours, in urine for up to twelve hours. But routine blood and urine screens do not detect it.[17] Undigested GHB may be found in a victim's vomit, too. And throwing up is a common effect of GHB.

Effects on the Body

Some people think GHB will make them feel drunk or happy. But it can knock them out and drag them close to death. One dose could make a person feel more talkative and eventually sleepy. Another dose might leave a person sick and dizzy and ready to vomit. A more potent dose can make someone feel like he or she has been hit over the head and gasping for breath. Since a person cannot predict how much GHB is in each dose, he or she is risking overdosing into coma or worse.

At very high doses, GHB can make a person feel very confused and enraged. Body temperatures can spike to high levels. A person could become temporarily paralyzed and lose control

GHB may make a person feel sick and dizzy.

of his bodily functions. Unable to wake up and go to the bathroom, he might wet himself during the night. Involuntary jerking of the head—an effect called the head snap—can happen within fifteen minutes of ingesting GHB. Several minutes of twitching, strange behavior, or blackouts are also common. Memory loss is a problem at any dose.[18]

Like alcohol, GHB depresses the central nervous system, which means it slows down the brain, heart rate, breathing, and other functions. But GHB does it more powerfully and rapidly than alcohol. People who mix the two are risking their life.

The time it takes for these effects to kick in can be anywhere from fifteen to thirty minutes. They typically last for three to six hours, but sometimes longer.[19] The same dose of GHB can have different effects in different people.[20] The dose that might make a 150-pound girl feel euphoric could knock out a 300-pound man— maybe even kill him.[21]

Personal and Social Aspects

Passing out while on GHB (or Rohypnol) is some- times called carpeting out, scooping out, or throwing down. In only minutes, a person can

Street names for GHB include: Liquid Ecstasy, Grievous Bodily Harm, Georgia Home Boy, Liquid X, Liquid E, Scoop, Salty Water, G-Riffick, Cherry Meth, Zonked, Organic Quaalude, G, Jib, GH Buddy, Aminos, and Everclear.[22]

lose control, forget what is happening, and fall unconscious.

Around the United States, some college students add GHB to beer, thinking they can get drunk for less money. At Florida State University, one junior said that GHB is "very popular. At clubs, they go around and sell it to you in a shot."[23] One of her friends uses it as an alternative to drinking when she goes out because she does not like the taste of alcohol.[24] Even if a person does not want GHB, someone may try to pass it off to her as an energy drink. Sometimes the drug leaves a residue in the glass or causes excessive foam, but otherwise is hard to detect. In the past ten years, GHB has become more widely available and more abused. People think it is harmless, but reports by the DEA and hospital emergency departments prove otherwise.[25]

CHAPTER FOUR

ROHYPNOL

Because it is inexpensive, Rohypnol became popular with high school and college students. Some took it to help them sleep; others heard it could make them feel drunk. Often it has been used in date rape. To address this, Congress passed the Drug-Induced Rape Prevention and Punishment Act of 1996.[1] Any person convicted of using the drug to aid in rape or any other violent crime may face a prison term of up to twenty years.[2]

Alicia* had just moved from the Midwest to go to San Diego State University. She rented an apartment in a bad section of town. But she felt a little safer sharing it with a young married couple. One of their neighbors, Vincent*, started hanging around and befriended Alicia. He was about twenty-five years old and came from an affluent family. Ever since getting out of the Navy, he had been running what he called an entertainment business. He organized parties.

"Alicia told me she thought he was nice look-ing, but just a friend. Nothing more," said Detective Sandra Oplinger of the San Diego Police Department's (SDPD) Sex Crimes Unit.[3] One night, Alicia and her roommates were having a little party. Vincent dropped by and said he would be right back with his specialty drink. He called it "pink panties." "He mixed vodka with pink lemonade in a blender," explained Oplinger. "But to Alicia, he said, 'I'll make a special one for you.' At the time, she didn't think much of it."[4]

Alicia did not remember much after taking

* Not their real names

just a few sips. "She drank half her drink and remembered trying to eat a cookie, but started drooling down the side of her mouth. So, she went to bed."[5] Next thing Alicia remembered was being very groggy and looking up to see Vincent on top of her. She fell in and out of consciousness. She woke up at noon the next day, still feeling sleepy. She had blood all over herself.

Her roommate drove her to the hospital. An emergency department doctor examined her. He took blood and urine samples, which would be tested for drugs, disease, and pregnancy. The

MYTH		FACT
If someone slipped a "roofie" into my drink, the drink would turn blue.	vs.	It might, now that Hoffmann-La Roche makes a new version of Rohypnol that turns a drink blue. But it would not be so obvious in a dark drink. Besides, the old pills that simply dissolve without a trace are still out there. Be alert.

doctor confirmed what Alicia feared: she had been raped.

Even though they would not get the test results for weeks, Oplinger notes, "based on her statement and the symptoms she described, I assumed she had been drugged."[6]

Several weeks later, the results from Alicia's blood and urine tests came in and proved Oplinger right. Alicia had had Rohypnol in her system. Alicia had never taken Rohypnol—or so she thought.

Oplinger discussed Alicia's case with another detective in her department. When she mentioned Vincent's name and his special drink, the colleague stopped her and said, "Wait a minute, I know that name,. . . and that drink."[7] It turns out the colleague had handled a similar case about nine months earlier. The victim had also been about seventeen years old, was a "friend" of Vincent, and drank his special drink. They did a little research and discovered a third victim with a similar profile, only she was nineteen years old.

"After identifying the suspect and interviewing the victim," says Oplinger, "I wrote a search warrant for the suspect's residence. He still lived in the same apartment complex as the victim."[8] Oplinger brought the warrant to the district attorney's office. They issued a rape charge, authorizing the SDPD to search Vincent's apartment. "On serving the search warrant, we found several pieces of evidence," continues Oplinger, "including growth-enhancing drugs and photographs of parties where girls were dancing naked and partially naked. We tagged the evidence and brought the suspect into custody."[10]

When questioned, Vincent claimed that it was not rape. He said that Alicia had consented to it. Though he had left the party earlier, he had broken back into the apartment through Alicia's bedroom window. He claimed she had let him in. When asked why, he maintained he was coming back to get his shoes.[11] "Now, why didn't he simply knock on the apartment door?" wondered Oplinger.[12]

Vincent had to undergo a psychiatric evaluation, which did not find anything wrong with him.

Meanwhile, his parents, who were very influential in the community, had started a letter-writing campaign in defense of their son. They did not believe he could do this sort of thing. When Vincent finally went before the judge, his charges were knocked down from rape to sexual battery with three years' probation. If he had been convicted of rape, he would have faced eight to twenty-five years behind bars.

History

Flunitrazepam, the active ingredient in Rohypnol, was developed as a sleeping aid in the late 1960s and early 1970s by the Swiss pharmaceutical company Hoffmann-La Roche, Inc. It was first sold under the trade name Rohypnol in 1975 in Switzerland, and used as an anesthetic (which numbs a person to pain) for surgery. Therapists began using it to relax patients and get them talking.[13] Around the same time, people were taking it illegally at parties and clubs throughout Europe.

Though illegal in the United States, it is smuggled in from Mexico and other countries where Rohypnol is legal. Since the mid-1980s, drug traffickers have spread Rohypnol to many countries. In May 1995, near London, England, authorities

Benzodiazepines

Though Rohypnol (flunitrazepam) is illegal in the United States, more than thirty other benzo-diazepines are legal. They have become part of the increasing problem of prescription drug abuse. Drug-treatment centers see teens get into trouble by combining and sharing their parents' medications with classmates. This is very dangerous. These medications are only safe when taken as prescribed by a doctor. The following is a partial list of the most commonly prescribed benzodiazepines.

Trade Name	Generic Name
Ativan	Lorazepam
Centrax	Prazepam
Dalmane	Flurazepam
Halcion	Triazolam
Klonopin	Clonazepam
Librium	Chlordiazepoxide
Prosom	Estazolam
Restoril	Temazepam
Tranxene	Clorazepate
Valium	Diazepam
Xanax	Alprazolam

seized a record one hundred-thousand Rohypnol tablets from the owner of a pharmaceutical dis- tributor. The investigation revealed that the pills had been manufactured in Belgium and were headed for Egypt. Many illegal loads of Rohypnol have been smuggled into the United States through Florida from Colombia and other Latin American countries. Suppliers use international mail, courier services, and passengers on com- mercial airlines. Texas has been another major entry point, largely due to smuggling by car and on foot across the U.S.–Mexico border.[14]

Chemical and Scientific Information

Rohypnol belongs to a class of drugs known as benzodiazepine, which is a kind of sedative (a drug that calms anxiety). But it is much more potent than most.[15] Benzodiazepines generally fall into two categories: they are either long last- ing (like Valium) or very strong (like Ativan). But Rohypnol is both.[16] In fact, it is ten times stronger than Valium.[17]

The traditional pills, commonly called Roofies, are round and white and somewhat smaller than aspirin. They are usually labeled "Roche" with a circled number 1 or 2.[18] To help prevent another person falling victim to a predator, Hoffmann-La Roche has made a new formulation of the drug that could be harder to abuse. The newer caplet is dull green with a blue core, imprinted with the number "542." It takes longer to dissolve and turns a drink blue.[19] People typically swallow the pill, but sometimes crush it into a powder and snort it. The powder can also be dissolved quickly in liquid and injected with a needle. Mixed in a drink, it has a bitter taste, but its taste can be mostly covered.

In the brain, the two most common neurotransmitters (chemical messengers) are GABA and glutamate. GABA is critical for the central nervous system, while glutamate plays a key role in learning and memory, among other functions.

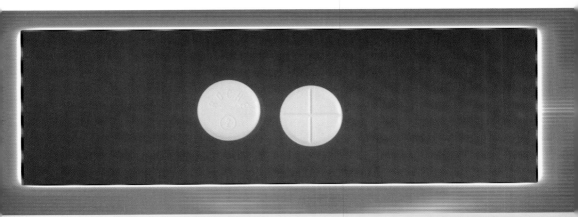

Rohypnol is a kind of sedative that is more potent than most others.

Rohypnol disrupts the important GABA neuro-transmitter, which can lead to coma and death.[20]

If Rohypnol does not kill, it still might knock someone unconscious. That is very dangerous, because anyone could be taken advantage of. Rohypnol can also produce a type of amnesia that causes a victim to forget what happened while under the effects of the drug. It can be detected in blood samples within twelve to twenty-four hours of taking it, and in urine within two to four days.[21]

Effects on the Body

Some people describe it as being hypnotized. Rohypnol can make them feel dizzy and confused right away. It eventually lowers blood pressure and makes them drowsy. If someone passes out, he or she may fall in and out of consciousness. But even when somewhat aware mentally, they can-not physically move or speak. Some victims have described it as being paralyzed, unable to move their arms or legs.[22]

Some people believe that Rohypnol is safe because it comes in pre-sealed bubble packs. They call it a cheap drunk and a cure for alcohol hangovers. If someone swallows too much

Rohypnol diluted in alcohol, he or she could fall into a coma. Though Rohypnol is a downer, it can make some people very aggressive. They might yell or physically lash out at their friends. The effects vary person to person, but the risk of ending the night in the hospital emergency department is constant.[23]

A person will start feeling the effects within twenty to thirty minutes of swallowing Rohypnol. Typically, that lasts from four to six hours, but some people have had these problems even twelve hours later.[24] Mixed in alcohol, Rohypnol works even faster. The combination is extremely dangerous—and could be deadly.

Personal and Social Aspects

"College students on spring break in Mexico will pick up Roofies," says Sean Collingsworth, a narcotics expert and twenty-year veteran of the Los Angeles Sheriff's Department.[25] "They bring it back over the border and pretty soon the drug's circulating campuses and clubs."[26] In fact, some pharmacies do not even ask for a prescription. Others might send a buyer to a doctor who will write a prescription for anything.[27]

For high school and college students who take

Some people may become aggressive after using Rohypnol and may lash out at their friends and family for no reason.

Rohypnol voluntarily, part of the appeal has been the drug's small size, which makes it easy to share and easy to hide. Since the government crackdown, many users have turned to other tranquilizers, such as Valium, Xanax, and Ativan.[28] But the DEA still sees Rohypnol crossing into Florida, Texas, and California—and to a lesser extent in New York, Minnesota, and elsewhere.[29]

CHAPTER FIVE

KETAMINE

The caged dogs were barking wildly. It was just after midnight in a Boston suburb, and Mike* was sneaking around an animal kennel that belonged to a local veterinarian. The fifteen year old was searching for a way to break in. He used a screwdriver to open a window

* Not his real name

in the kennel, and then made his way to the veterinarian's office.[1]

Inside the office, he quickly found the cabinet containing vials of ketamine. It was locked, so Mike broke it open with a small pry bar he had brought with him. He loaded as many boxes of vials as he could into his backpack and turned to leave. Just as he reached the back door, Mike heard police sirens blaring down the street. A silent alarm had alerted the cops to a break-in. Mike thought about hiding in the kennel, but he knew the dogs would give him away. He broke into a run and headed for the woods behind the kennel. But it was too late. The police were already in the driveway and they had spotted him.[2]

Mike ran several feet before being tackled by an officer. The officer twisted Mike's arms behind his back and fastened handcuffs on his wrists. The other officer called for a police wagon to take Mike to the station. While they waited, more officers arrived at the scene.

At the station, Mike was fingerprinted and photographed. He was put in a cell by himself. One of the officers called his parents. When

Mike's mother arrived, the officer told her that her son had been arrested for breaking and entering, possession of a controlled substance (drug regulated by the government), and larceny. The officer asked Mike a lot of questions about what he had done, but the teen did not say much. He was released and allowed to go home with his mother, but he had to appear in court the next day.

When Mike and his mother got to juvenile court, they were told to wait in a hallway, where other kids were sitting with their parents. Just after lunch, Mike's case was called. The judge asked him to explain himself. Mike took responsibility for breaking in, because he had been caught in the act. The judge gave him a lecture about respecting others and their property. The judge said she was very worried about the amount of ketamine he had attempted to steal and the potential consequences that users might suffer. Her court was more troubled about suppliers and dealers, she said, than it was about the users. Suppliers meant more harm to more people. And considering the amount he tried to steal, Mike would have been a major supplier.[4]

Because it was his first offense, Mike was put on probation for twelve months and had to do community service. While on probation, he had to meet with his probation officer, Paul Keefe, twice a month and undergo regular drug tests. "The very first time, he tested positive for marijuana," says Keefe. "So he was put on a weekly drug-testing schedule."[5] He also had to spend one Saturday per month doing community service with other kids under the supervision of their probation officers.

Community service meant eight hours each Saturday. "One Saturday," notes Keefe, "we were working on the *USS Salem*, a huge, decommissioned Navy destroyer ship."[6] Mike was part of a group who had to clean the crew's quarters and set up the ship for a Veterans Day ceremony. Amid the highly decorated officers and honor guard, "you could tell Mike felt self-conscious," continued Keefe. "This was a big ceremony, and lots of people saw him. Some of his friends knew he had been arrested, but now everyone knew—including his former little league and basketball coaches."[7] Mike tried to make up an excuse, but it was clear why he was there.[8] The probation officers all wore jackets that read "PROBATION" in big block letters on the back.

"He wanted the judge to let him do his community service at the kennel," says Keefe. "But the owner didn't want Mike anywhere near the animals or his drug cabinet."[9] In fact, the owner had requested that the judge order him to stay away from the kennel for a year. "And," exclaims Keefe, "this was the vet that Mike's mother brought their dog to!"[10]

"When I asked him why he had stolen the ketamine," explains Keefe, "Mike told me that he had seen a television show in which one of the investigators had been injected with Special K."[11] The episode went on to describe how ketamine was used at raves and clubs. "Mike figured if there was a market for K, then he could make a lot of money selling it."[12]

History

Ketamine is a hallucinogen. The word *hallucinogen* comes from the Latin word *alucinare*, which means "to wander in mind and talk idly."[13] Made popular in the 1960s by beatniks and hippies, hallucinogens are a family of drugs that includes the painkiller phencyclidine (PCP), also called angel dust. Because PCP caused intense and scary hallucinations, researchers began looking for a safer alternative. In 1962, pharmacist Calvin Stevens found a solution when he synthesized Ketamine Hydrochloride for Parke-Davis Laboratories.[14] Still, after further testing, researchers found it to be a potent psychedelic drug. Psychedelic means that a person may feel that his mind is detached from his body.

In 1966, Parke-Davis patented ketamine as an

anesthetic, and it became widely used during the Vietnam War (1957–1975) to treat wounded soldiers. In 1969, ketamine became available by prescription only under the name Ketalar.[15] In the early 1970s, veterinarians used it as an animal tranquilizer. But illegal use was also growing throughout the world. By the late 1990s, ketamine had become increasingly popular among high-school ravers. But, as with GHB and Rohypnol, ketamine also has been used in date rape. Ketamine is included in the Drug-Induced Rape Prevention Act of 1996. In 1999, it was added to the list of illegal drugs regulated by the Controlled Substance Act. It is illegal to possess ketamine without a license or prescription.[16]

Suppliers of club drugs have been a major focus for the Drug Enforcement Administration in recent years. In fall of 2002, the DEA shut down an international ketamine distribution ring in South Florida.[17] The two-year investigation, known as Operation Ravemaker, ended with agents arresting eight men. They had been smuggling thousands of vials of ketamine from Mexico to California, Florida, and New York. By intercepting cellular phone calls, agents located and

Protect Yourself

Take responsibility for your safety. Do the best you can to avoid being slipped any drugs.

1. At parties, check in with friends every twenty minutes.

2. Before leaving the party, let your friends know where you are going and with whom.

3. Do not take drinks from someone you do not know well and trust.

4. Consider bringing your own drinks in containers that are securely covered.

5. Always open your own drinks if they are offered by someone else.

6. Do not accept drinks from a punch bowl.

7. Never leave your drink unattended. If you go to the bathroom, take it with you. If you get up to dance, finish it or take it with you.

8. Do not share or exchange drinks.

9. Do not drink anything that has a funny smell, color, or taste.

10. If you start to feel numb or like you might pass out, tell your friends immediately. They should call 911.

seized 1,350 vials being sent from Mexico to South Florida. As the investigation progressed, it became clear that in addition to drug trafficking, these men were also actively involved in credit-card fraud. DEA agents served the ringleader with a search warrant at his home in Miami Beach, Florida. They took possession of eight stolen luxury cars valued at nearly half-million dollars—including three Mercedes Benzes, two Corvettes, and a Jaguar. Among the weapons agents found were two shotguns, two AK–47 semi-automatic assault rifles, one rifle, and two revolvers. They also seized two dozen credit cards and more than three dozen fake identification cards to match the credit cards—along with two hundred more vials of ketamine.[18]

Chemical and Scientific Information

Ketamine is made by pharmaceutical companies. It makes its way to the street, where it is often called Special K, through theft and illegal prescriptions. It comes in a powder or liquid. People sometimes evaporate the liquid on a hot plate, a warming tray, or in a microwave oven to produce crystals. They then grind the crystals into powder.

Powdered ketamine is cut into lines known as bumps and snorted. It is also added to marijuana or tobacco and smoked. People sometimes press the powder into tablets with ecstasy, and swallow the combination. Liquid ketamine is injected straight into muscles or mixed into drinks.[19] The drug is sold in different packages. Sometimes, it comes in small glass vials or plastic bags; other times it can come in capsules or in folded-up paper or aluminum foil.[20]

Though ketamine is milder than PCP in its effects on the brain, it can still make someone feel very disconnected from everyone and everything around him.[21] It is used legally by veterinarians to sedate cats, monkeys, and other animals for surgery. On humans, ketamine is used very rarely in emergency surgery for burn victims and on the battlefield. Surgeons do not like to use it on people, because patients have awoken after surgery with terrifying hallucinations.[22]

Ketamine and PCP have been used to study schizophrenia, a brain disorder. Both drugs cause many of the same symptoms as schizophrenia, so researchers are examining the drugs' effects on the brain to better understand how schizophrenia works. With their findings, they hope to develop more effective treatments for the disorder.[23]

Ketamine is a complicated drug, because it has so many different effects on brain activity. It is a depressant, like alcohol, which can make people clumsy and slur their speech. As a stimulant, it raises a person's blood pressure and body temperature. And like an analgesic, which is a pain

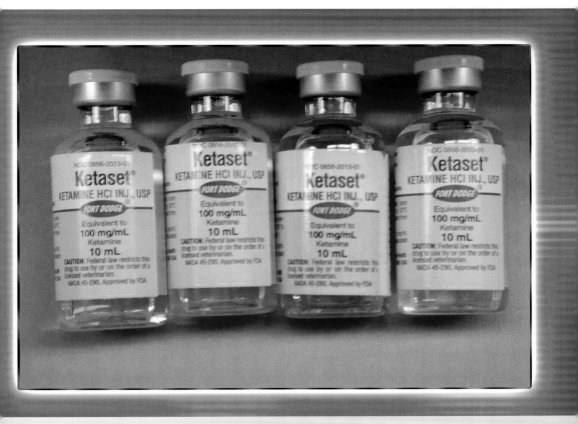

Veterinarians legally used ketamine to sedate animals in their care for surgery. However, when people take this drug it raises blood pressure, makes people feel disconnected, and some-times abusers will not know where they are.

reliever, ketamine makes people less sensitive to pain. All that happening at once means users might not be aware that they are hurting themselves or someone else—until it is too late.[24]

In the brain, ketamine blocks the neurotransmitter glutamate at its receptors—where drugs attach to nerve cells.[25] This blockade is what causes someone to have visions and feel like his mind is separated from his body. Because ketamine works on the same receptor as alcohol, combining the two is very dangerous. It increases the chance of dying through respiratory depression, which means the brain forgets to tell the lungs to breathe.

Ketamine moves through the body much more quickly than GHB or Rohypnol. Taking effect within twenty minutes, ketamine's high can last up to ninety minutes. The drug is difficult to detect, but some advanced tests have been developed specifically for ketamine. If tested within forty-eight hours of taking it, ketamine can be found in blood and urine samples.[26]

When someone is arrested carrying drugs, police detectives need to test the drugs to determine which type they are. Some drug samples can

Protect Your Friends

Slipping a drug into a drink and assaults are a risk at a party or any place where people are gathered. It is a good idea to make a pact with your friends beforehand to ensure everyone's safety.

1. Keep your friends close by, in your sight, if possible.

2. Watch your friends' behavior for anything out of the ordinary.

3. If they seem intoxicated when they did not drink alcohol, they could be in trouble.

4. If they seem confused or physically weak, they could be in trouble.

5. If you see or hear that someone is drugging a drink or a punch bowl, warn others.

6. If you hear someone even kidding about date-rape drugs, pay attention. Warn others and leave that party.

7. Tell your friends about the high-risk places and situations where these drugs have been known to be used.

8. If one of your friends appears very unstable, gets sick after drinking a beverage, or seems to have difficulty breathing, help her to a safe place. If necessary, call 911 for emergency medical assistance.

9. Save any potential evidence such as the glass or can that held her drink.

10. At the hospital, tell the doctor about drugs you think your friend may have been given.

be tested in the field, but all ultimately go to the police department's narcotics lab.

"We get ketamine either in bottles or as a white powder in a little plastic bag," explains Steve Cordes, a drug analyst with the San Diego Police Department in California.[27] If it is in a bottle, the analysts check the label for manufacturer, which they can contact for more information about that particular batch of ketamine. Then they run the drug through the gas chromatograph mass spectrometer (GCMS). About the same size as a large microwave oven, the GCMS breaks down drug samples into fragments of known drug groups. "We analyze those fragments and check for patterns unique to each drug," says Cordes. "Then we run those patterns against our computer database until it finds a match."[28] Such testing may provide enough evidence for officers to hold a suspect and bring the case to trial.

Effects on the Body

Some users hallucinate, imagining things are there that really are not. Others have described it as like watching themselves in a dream. While ketamine does not always cause hallucinations, people usually see some sort of distortion. A person might be sitting on the ground and feel that the boundary between the ground and his body no longer exists.[29] They might feel as if they are falling or being sucked down into a tunnel. Users have described it as "your body disappears and you are just a head rolling along."[30] "Going down into a K-hole" is how they describe this feeling of being cut off from reality.

A serious risk with ketamine is lowered inhibitions. An inhibition is what stops us from doing things that we normally would not do. Under the influence of ketamine, for example, someone may do something life threatening like run into traffic. An overdose of ketamine will knock a person out as if in an operating room. If a person takes large doses of it repeatedly, he or she could not only black out but have a heart attack and die.

The hallucinatory effects of ketamine are relatively short acting. They kick in within twenty minutes and last about an hour or so. But a person's feelings, senses, judgment, and coordination may be affected for up to twenty-four hours.[31]

Another problem with ketamine can be flashbacks. A person may suddenly recall something that happened while on the drug. The flashback

Ketamine may cause people to do things they may not normally do, like drive recklessly.

may be a hallucination. It may or may not have really happened, but feels as if it did. Though more of a problem for people who take it regularly, this can happen after using ketamine only once—especially if it was mixed with alcohol.[32]

Personal and Social Aspects

There are those who take ketamine regularly, because they believe it will expand their mind and give them a deeper understanding of themselves and the world. "They often claim to have lofty goals, like self-exploration and enhancing their consciousness," finds Dr. Stalcup, medical director of a California drug treatment center. Such users rarely think it is addictive, he adds.[33]

Because the process for making ketamine is so complex and time-consuming, kitchen chemists do not typically try to make it. People usually get it from friends at nightclubs, private parties, and raves. Dealers get it by stealing from a veterinary office or by smuggling it into the country. From Mexico, a common source, couriers sneak over the border into the United States on foot or in private cars. Other illegal supplies come in by mail from South America and Europe.[34]

CHAPTER SIX

TREATMENT

GHB

As a former narcotics detective and current club-drug consultant, Trinka Porrata has encountered hundreds of people who have struggled with GHB addiction. "This is one terrifying drug," says Porrata.[1] Through Web sites, Porrata and others have helped people addicted to GHB get treatment. "I have detoxed addicts who remain terrified of what long-term damage they have done."[2]

Because of the drug, children have found their father passed out naked in the front room, urinating all over himself, or passed out in the car—or, worse, passed out while driving with the children in the car.[3] One woman in California "started videotaping her husband's bizarre incidents."[4] She woke up early one morning and he was not in bed. After searching inside and out, Porrata writes, "she found him asleep in the middle of the street in front of their house. She videotaped that and showed him the tape. He dumped more than seventy bottles of GHB that he had stashed and went to the emergency room for withdrawal."[5] He went from the psychiatric ward to intensive care for several days, strapped down for most of them. He remembered very little of it, but he hallucinated that he was strapped to the deck of a ship adrift at sea for days.

Another man, a bodybuilder, started using GBL, one of GHB's chemical cousins. "The impact was awesome," he said.[6] He felt he could see muscle gain and fat loss happen immediately.[7] He no longer felt sleepy during the day. But soon enough, there were warning signs. A few times, he stopped breathing at night and woke up in a panic, trying to force himself to breathe regularly again. While brushing his teeth, he occasionally smacked his forehead against the mirror. He crashed into a couple of things, breaking off the oven door handle as he passed by. These things happened because of a common GHB side effect called the head snap, in which users jerk their heads involuntarily.

After nine months of use, he was taking GBL day and night. Then one day he took a combination of vitamins and supplements, but did not take his usual dose of GBL. "He suddenly began sweating in a most unusual way," notes Porrata. "The palms of his hands and soles of his feet were oozing a thick, waxy sweat. His heart was racing. His blood pressure soared."[8] Blaming it on the combination of supplements, he continued taking GBL.

"GHB proponents love to claim that only the irresponsible users, the ravers, the careless,. . . fall victim to any problems with GHB," says Porrata. This bodybuilder thought the same.

"And then he skipped the usual dose of G. The withdrawal symptoms began. . . He also noticed that if you put BD—another GHB cousin that he had been using interchangeably with GBL—in a Styrofoam cup, it ate the Styrofoam. He now wondered what it might be doing to his body."[9]

Once he realized he was addicted, he tried to quit.

"He said he dreaded every drink of GHB and was gradually cutting back . . . he had not told me that he had barely been out in public (or even in his gym) for weeks. He was becoming quite introverted and experiencing bizarre behavior."[10] His wife finally called 911, and he was rushed to the hospital in an ambulance. The doctor put him through three days of detoxification to get the drug out of his system. The hospital then released him with a prescription for medication. Fortunately, the medication worked well, keeping him relatively foggy and calm for eight to ten days. It kept him from having hallucinations and wild behavior that many addicts experience during this phase. He said he felt incredibly better to be free of GBL, but was frustrated by the sense of "doom and gloom" he felt. A few months later, the depression dwindled, but he still had difficulty sleeping.

"Bodybuilders are the ones more likely to become addicted, since they are most likely to take it on a regular basis," notes Porrata.[11] The same goes for people who use GHB frequently as an antidepressant or a sleep aid. There are many who initially used it only at raves or clubs, but soon developed addictions as well.

According to Porrata, most GHB users initially think the drug is great. They sleep well, become more outgoing, gain muscle tone. "And then one day it turns on you," she says. "It can be just two months or a few years before they realize that they are in trouble."[12] Most users realized they were addicted after four months to a year of taking GHB. "This does not mean that they weren't having trouble before that," Porrata warns. "Because of the dissociation, they do not realize when the trouble begins. They typically have episodes that they don't remember."[13] Interviews with roommates, spouses, friends, even their children prove that the troubles started much earlier. Once GHB reverses on them, they typically gain weight and are unable to discipline themselves to keep up their workout schedule. They become introverted and unable to deal with the public. Porrata tells of one young man in Oregon who had not been out of his house for more than three weeks and was paying a neighbor to bring him groceries.[14] Many have psychotic episodes and are unable to sleep.

GHB, over time, can lead to physical and psychological addiction. People who use it regularly will eventually need larger doses to get high. One psychiatrist described a typical scenario.[15] A person starts out using it for the drunk-like high. Then, one night, he has trouble falling asleep and turns to GHB for help. After doing that a few times, he reaches the point of using the drug every few hours, twenty-four hours a day, seven days a week. In that state, he can sleep no more than two to four hours before needing more GHB.

When users try to quit, the withdrawal process for this kind of dependency is incredibly difficult. Within two to three hours of stopping GHB, they will not be able to sleep and will feel extremely anxious. After the strange thick, waxy sweating, they will feel sick, heart rate and blood pressure will soar, and the body may jerk uncontrollably.

The first two or three days are most critical in terms of medical issues. After a few days, a person may seem all right, the patient may talk in complete sentences and say the right things to doctors. But he or she is far from OK.

The next eight to twelve days mean a new phase of withdrawal. High anxiety kicks in, along with hallucinations and days without sleep, which will only make the hallucinations worse. During this phase, the patient may not recognize friends or family and may say crazy and hurtful things. After this, he or she should feel better, but will likely feel depressed. It may take weeks or even months before this passes. The recovering addict still may have difficulty putting thoughts and sentences together. But about thirty to forty-five days later, this often improves significantly.[16]

Porrata notes, "The most important thing is supervision and support for at least two weeks, followed by ongoing counseling and monitoring."[17] Some people feel suicidal. Others have said that they truly could understand committing suicide while addicted to GHB and while trying

Finding friends or an adult you trust can be helpful in fighting addiction.

to detox.[18] The levels of pain and anxiety are incredible. Some addicts get over this after many months, others may take years.

Rohypnol

Though addiction to Rohypnol is not as common as GHB, it does happen. Neither is approved for sale or use in the United States, but Rohypnol is more difficult to get. And people can switch to other, more accessible benzodiazepines for similar effects.[19] Still, those who do take Rohypnol regularly can become addicted even after just a few weeks.[20] As time goes on, they need more of the drug to get the same high.

When addicts try to quit and Rohypnol starts to leave the body, they will go through withdrawal symptoms. Severe headaches, sore muscles, even hallucinations are common. They may also feel extremely anxious and confused. Some people have convulsions and seizures one to two weeks after quitting Rohypnol.

"Anxiety and insomnia are the most frequently seen symptoms," reports Dr. Alex Stalcup, medical director of a drug-treatment center in California. "Seizures, though rare, can be fatal."[21] But, Stalcup also notes that these symptoms can be prevented.

Quitting abruptly is dangerous, because the body has adapted to Rohypnol's effects. That is why an addict should get medical help. According to Stalcup, "Detoxification from benzodiazepines, when done properly, is a big deal. It requires medical supervision and skillful use of medications."[22]

Treatment can take several weeks to months. The type and amount of medication given depends on the particular patient. "The general approach is called substitute-taper," says Stalcup. "First, we substitute a long-acting sedative hypnotic, like phenobarbital, for the benzodiazepine. Some [doctors] substitute with valium or librium."[23] Patients are given the same dose per day until their vital signs (heart rate, blood pressure) return to normal and their withdrawal symptoms are under control. Then, a taper begins, which means that, over time, the dosage will be gradually reduced until those symptoms go away. "The patient's own comfort level guides the frequency with which we reduce the taper," notes Stalcup. "With this approach, symptom control is excellent and relapse is uncommon."[24]

Ketamine

"Most addicts become disenchanted with ketamine after they hit a K-hole," says Stalcup. "It can be so horrifying that they seek treatment."[25] For many, the K-hole is terrifying, because it makes them feel as if they are witnessing their own death.

Stalcup notes that treating ketamine addiction is very difficult. During withdrawal, the relatively mild symptoms include short-term memory loss, vision problems, and difficulty paying attention. More severe are the psychological effects, such as intense hallucinations.[26] Some people start to see patterns and coincidences around them that make them believe they are more important to the world than other people. The same delusion can make them paranoid.[27] "We have found that ketamine addicts often have an underlying mental illness," says Stalcup. "During withdrawal, that

MYTH   FACT

MYTH		FACT
Most drug addicts are low-lifes who live on the street.	vs.	Drug dependence shows no favorites. The majority of users come from all walks of life. There are children, men, and women—from farming communities to wealthy suburbs to the inner city—who use and abuse drugs.

illness begins to surface and is much worse than before they started ketamine."[28]

The mental health disorders that often underlie ketamine use tend to be serious, from severe depression to psychotic disorders. They each require aggressive medical treatment, which includes medication and counseling. Otherwise, patients will likely relapse, which means they go back to using the drug.

"We initially give them benzodiazepine (tranquilizer) to suppress ketamine withdrawal symptoms," notes Stalcup.[29]

Over the course of several weeks or months, the amount of tranquilizer given is gradually reduced. The time it takes for withdrawal symptoms to fade depends on the individual. But it is important to limit the use of benzodiazepines to short-term use. If given longer than a few weeks, the risk of the patient becoming dependent on them increases. The tranquilizer is given in even smaller doses, because stopping them abruptly or too soon can cause seizures. It is a delicate balance the doctor has to watch.

It is not easy to treat. "But, properly done," says Stalcup, "things can turn out okay."[30]

Treating Victims of Sexual Assault

Because GHB, Rohypnol, and ketamine have been used in sexual assault, it is important to point out that traumatized victims also need treatment to heal. They need help dealing with feelings of fear, loss of control, and depression severe enough to become suicidal. Many victims feel guilt and blame themselves. They think, "Why me?" Experts explain that this is their way of trying to understand an event that the victim had no control over. Blaming themselves is an attempt to take control. But a victim of sexual assault is never to blame.[31]

Victims of sexual assault in which drugs were used have additional trauma to overcome. They suffer the same horror as any rape victim, as well as prolonged helplessness at not being able to remember what was done to them. They can only imagine what happened. Such victims describe it as "mind rape."[32]

"Rape leaves a victim feeling dirty and used," reports Stalcup. "Drug-facilitated assault makes her mistrustful. She questions her own worth and judgment."[33]

Individual therapy can help victims learn to cope with such issues. There are also rape support groups, in which victims come together to share their fears, anger, and depression. By discussing it with other victims, they feel less isolated and gain confidence that they can put their life back together.

Overcoming addiction is extremely difficult. People addicted to these three drugs cannot

Finding a friend to talk to during a difficult and stressful time can help you through anything.

recover without treatment. Those who work with addicts agree on two general points: Relapse is typical, maybe even necessary for recovery; and support groups are essential.

People take drugs because they make them feel good—for a while. But someone can become addicted without even realizing it. Then it becomes a lifelong battle. That is where support groups can be especially helpful. Narcotics Anonymous is an organization that helps people find support groups. At group meetings, former drug users help each other in their struggle to stay drug free. Support from family and friends is another key part of the recovery process.

"When I ask the teens I'm treating why they used a drug," says Stalcup, "they say things like 'my friend tried it, and nothing happened to her.'"[34] Stalcup has been treating people with addiction for decades. He has seen how unpredictable drugs can be—and how difficult it is for people to recover from addiction.

The question he always asks is, "Is it worth the risk?"[35]

GLOSSARY

amnesia—Memory loss.

analgesic—A drug that reduces pain.

anesthetic—A drug that numbs a person to pain, typically given before surgery.

aphrodisiac—A substance that increases sexual desire.

autopsy—An examination and dissection of the body, done by a pathologist, to determine cause of death.

compound—A substance made up of two or more elements.

controlled substance—Drugs that the government closely regulates from manufacturing to selling.

downers—Another name for depressants, which are drugs that slow down the central nervous system (brain, heart rate, breathing, and other critical functions).

felony—A serious crime, such as murder or armed robbery, that carries severe punishment.

GABA—The neurotransmitter gamma-aminobutyric acid, which carries chemical messages between brain cells that are critical to the central nervous system.

glutamate—Neurotransmitter in the brain that is critical for learning, memory, and brain development.

hallucination—Imagining things are there that really are not; they exist only in the person's mind.

larceny—Crime involving the stealing of someone else's possessions.

mandatory—Required by a regulation or law.

manslaughter—Unintentional murder, in which death occurs through recklessness or neglect.

misdemeanor—A crime, such as trespassing or vandalism, that is less serious than a felony and carries lighter punishment than a felony.

neurotransmitter—A chemical that carries messages between brain cells. GABA and glutamate are the two most common neurotransmitters in the brain.

overdose—Taking more of a drug than the body can tolerate, which can lead to uncontrollable spasms, unconsciousness, coma, and death.

sedative—A drug that calms or tranquilizes, useful for people who suffer from severe anxiety.

synthesized—Made by a person, rather than found in nature. Pharmaceutical companies synthesize drugs from various chemicals.

trance—A half-conscious state, somewhere between sleeping and waking, in which a person's attention is narrowly focused. In a trance state, a person may lose the ability to function voluntarily, as if hypnotized.

CHAPTER NOTES

Chapter 1. Predatory Drugs

1. J. S. Cohen, "Trendy Drug Shatters Hopes, Dreams, Innocence," *The Detroit News*, December 5, 1999, <http://www.detnews.com/specialreports/1999/ghb/sunlead/sunlead.htm> (November 15, 2004).
2. Ibid.
3. Ibid.
4. Ibid.
5. "The Dawn Report: Club Drugs, 2002 Update," July 2004, <http://oas.samhsa.gov/2k4/clubdrugs.pdf> (September 2005).
6. Ibid.
7. "Gamma Hydroxybutyrate (GHB)," November 2002, <http://www.whitehousedrugpolicy.gov/publications/factsht/gamma/index.html> (November 20, 2004).
8. "Club Drugs," *SAMSHA News*, vol. X, No. 3, Summer 2002, <http://alt.samhsa.gov/SAMHSA_news/Summer2002/text_only/article11txt.htm> (January 12, 2005).
9. M. LeBeau, A. Mozayani, et al., *Drug-Facilitated Sexual Assault: A Forensic Handbook* (San Diego: Academic Press, 2001), p. 101.
10. "The Dawn Report: Club Drugs, 2002 Update."
11. "Emergency Department Trends from the Drug Abuse Warning Network, Final Estimates

1995–2002," Office of Applied Studies, SAMH-SA (September 2005).

12. "The Dawn Report: Club Drugs, 2002 Update."
13. "Drug Facts: Club Drugs," n.d., <http://www.whitehousedrugpolicy.gov/drugfact/club/index.html> (November 20, 2004).
14. "The Dawn Report: Club Drugs, 2002 Update."

Chapter 2. Background Information

1. M. LeBeau and A. Mozayani, eds., *Drug-Facilitated Sexual Assault: A Forensic Handbook* (San Diego: Academic Press, 2001), p. 79.
2. "The Dawn Report: Benzodiazepines in Drug Abuse-Related Emergency Department Visits: 1995–2002," April 2004, <http://www.samhsa.gov/2k4benzodiazepinesTrends.pdf> (September 2005).
3. Personal interview with Dr. Alex Stalcup, medical director, New Lease Treatment Center, California, September 14, 2005.
4. "Drugs History," University of Minnesota, Morris, n.d., <http://www.morris.edu/~ratliffj/psy1081> (November 8, 2004).
5. "History of Heroin and Opium Timeline," Narconon, Arrowhead (OK), n.d., <http://www.heroinaddiction.com/heroin_timeline.html> (November 8, 2004).
6. Ibid.
7. "DEA History Book: 1970–1975," The Drug

Enforcement Administration, n.d., <http://www.usdoj.gov/dea/pubs/history/deahistory_01.htm#1> (November 10, 2004).

8. "History of the Anti-Saloon League 1893–1933," Westerville Public Library (OH), n.d., <http://www.wpl.lib.oh.us/AntiSaloon/history/> (November 8, 2004).

9. Richard J. Bonnie and Charles H. Whitebread, II, "The Forbidden Fruit and the Tree of Knowledge: An Inquiry Into the Legal History of American Marijuana Prohibition," *Virginia Law Review*, vol. 56, October 1970, <http://www.druglibrary.org/schaffer/LIBRARY/studies/vlr/vlrtoc.htm> (November 10, 2004).

10. "DEA History Book: 1970–1975," The Drug Enforcement Administration.

11. Ibid.

12. C. Kuhn, et al., *Buzzed: The Straight Facts About the Most Used and Abused Drugs From Alcohol to Ecstasy*, 2d ed. (New York: W.W. Norton & Co., 2003), p. 75.

13. "Audit Report: Department of Justice Drug Demand Reduction Activities," February 2003, <http://www.usdoj.gov/oig/audit/plus/0312/intro.htm> (November 13, 2004).

14. Physican's Manual—Outline of Controlled Substances Act of 1970, n.d., <http://www.vetmed.wsu.edu/pharmacy/vm522p/dea_all.htm> (February 7, 2005).

15. "DEA History Book: 1970–1975," The Drug Enforcement Administration.

16. "Fact Sheet: Rohypnol," Office of National Drug Control Policy, February 2003, <http://www.whitehousedrugpolicy.gov/publications/factsht/rohypnol/index/html> (September 15, 2005).

17. L. D. Johnston, P. M. O'Malley, et al., *Monitoring the Future national results on adolescent drug use, 2004* (Bethesda, Md.: National Institute on Drug Abuse, 2005).

18. Ibid.

19. "NIDA InfoFacts: Club Drugs," n.d., <http://www.drugabuse.gov/Infofax/Clubdrugs.html> (December 10, 2004).

20. Personal interview with Richard Woodfork, DEA–New Orleans, March 22, 2005.

21. Ibid.

22. "In the Spotlight: Club Drugs—Summary," National Criminal Justice Reference Service, n.d., <http://www.ncjrs.org/club_drugs/summary.html> (December 10, 2004).

Chapter 3. GHB

1. T. Nordenberg, "The Death of the Party: All the Rave, GHB's Hazards Go Unheeded," *FDA Consume Magazine*, March–April 2000, <http://www.fda.gov/fdac/features/2000/200_ghb.html> (January 11, 2004).

2. A. Shortidge, "Caleb Shortridge, Our Son and

Friend," May 1, 1998, <http://www.trendydrugs. org/tragic.htm> (January 11, 2004).

3. N. Fitzgerald and K. J. Riley, "Drug-Facilitated Rape: Looking for the Missing Pieces," *National Institute of Justice Journal*, April 2000.

4. "What is GHB?" n.d., <http://www.projectghb. org/english.htm> (November 9, 2004).

5. Personal interview with Trinka Porrata, club-drug consultant and former narcotics detective, Los Angeles Police Department, September 9, 2005.

6. "GHB & GHB Analogs," n.d., <http://www. streetdrugs.org/ghb.htm> (November 9, 2004).

7. Ibid.

8. M. LeBeau and A. Mozayani, eds., *Drug-Facilitated Sexual Assault: A Forensic Handbook* (San Diego: Academic Press, 2001), Preface.

9. J. S. Cohen, "Trendy Drug Shatters Hopes, Dreams, Innocence," *The Detroit News*, December 5, 1999, <http://www.detnews. com/specialreports/1999/ghb/sunlead/ sunlead.htm> (November 15, 2004).

10. *Drug Facilitated Sexual Assault Resource Guide*, National Drug Intelligence Center and George Mason University, Alexandria, Virginia, May 2003, p. 4.

11. "Operation Webslinger," September 19, 2002, <www.dea.gov/pubs/pressrel/pr091902p. html> (March 11, 2005).

12. Ibid.

13. "A Deadly Trip," *NewsHour Extra: Date-Rape Drugs*, April 11, 2000, <http://www.pbs.org/newshour/extra/features/jan-june00/ghb.html> (November 29, 2004).
14. C. Kuhn, et al., *Buzzed: The Straight Facts About the Most Used and Abused Drugs From Alcohol to Ecstasy*, 2d ed. (New York: W.W. Norton & Co., 2003), pp. 200–201.
15. M. LeBeau and A. Mozayani, p. 112.
16. Ibid., p. 116.
17. Kuhn, et al., p. 201.
18. Personal interview with Trinka Porrata.
19. "Drug Facts: Club Drugs," n.d., <http://www.whitehousedrugpolicy.gov/drugfact/club/index.html> (November 20, 2004).
20. Dr. E. S. Rome, "It's a Rave New World: Rave Culture and Illicit Drug Use in the Young," *Cleveland Clinic Journal of Medicine*, vol. 68, no. 6, June 2001, p. 545.
21. T. Nordenberg, "The Death of the Party: All the Rave, GHB's Hazards Go Unheeded."
22. Ibid.
23. *Drug Facilitated Sexual Assault Resource Guide*, p. 4.
24. Ibid.
25. "The Dawn Report: Club Drugs, 2002 Update," July 2004, <http://www.samhsa.gov/oas/DAWN.htm> (September 2005); and "Intelligence Bulletin: GHB Trafficking and Abuse," September 2004. n.d., <http://www.

usdoj.gov/ndic/pubs10/10331/index.htm>
(December 4, 2004).

Chapter 4. Rohypnol

1. "InfoFacts: Club Drugs," National Institute on Drug Abuse, n.d., <http://www.nida.nih.gov/Infofax/RohypnolGHB.html> (November 12, 2004).
2. "Intelligence Bulletin: Ketamine," National Drug Intelligence Center, July 2004, <http://www.usdoj.gov/ndic/pubs10/10255/index.htm> (November 12, 2004).
3. Personal interview with Detective Sandra Oplinger, San Diego Police Department, March 23, 2005.
4. Ibid.
5. Ibid.
6. Ibid.
7. Ibid.
8. Ibid.
9. *Drug Facilitated Sexual Assault Resource Guide*, p. 7.
10. Personal Interview with Detective Sandra Oplinger.
11. Ibid.
12. Ibid.
13. "Abuse and Trafficking of Rohypnol," DEA Congressional Testimony by Terrance W. Woodworth, Deputy Director, Office of Diversion Control, DEA, July 16, 1996,

<http://www.usdoj.gov/dea/pubs/cngrtest/ct960516.htm> (November 12, 2004).

14. Ibid.

15. C. Kuhn, et al., *Buzzed: The Straight Facts About the Most Used and Abused Drugs From Alcohol to Ecstasy*, 2d ed. (New York: W.W. Norton & Co., 2003), pp. 196–199.

16. Personal interview with Dr. Alex Stalcup, medical director, New Lease Treatment Center, California, September 14, 2005.

17. "Abuse and Trafficking of Rohypnol," July 16, 1996.

18. "What is Rohypnol?" n.d., <http://www.intheknowzone.com/DRdrugs/r_what.htm> (January 13, 2005).

19. "Rohypnol Fast Facts," August 2003, <http://www.usdoj.gov/ndic/pubs6/6074/index.htm> (November 29, 2004).

20. Kuhn, et al., pp. 196–199, 238.

21. *Drug Facilitated Sexual Assault Resource Guide*, National Drug Intelligence Center and George Mason University, Alexandria, Virginia, May 2003, p. 8.

22. N. Fitzgerald and K. J. Riley, "Drug-Facilitated Rape: Looking for the Missing Pieces," *National Institute of Justice Journal*, April 2000.

23. Dr. E. S. Rome, "It's a Rave New World: Rave Culture and Illicit Drug Use in the Young," *Cleveland Clinic Journal of Medicine*, vol. 68, no. 6, June 2001, p. 547.

24. "Drug Facts: Club Drugs," n.d., <http://

www.whitehousedrugpolicy.gov/drugfact/club/ index.html> (November 20, 2004).

25. Personal interview with Sean Collingsworth, narcotics expert, November 16, 2004.

26. Ibid.

27. Personal interview with Trinka Porrata, club-drug consultant and former narcotics detective, Los Angeles Police Department, September 9, 2005.

28. Personal interview with Dr. Alex Stalcup.

29. "State Factsheets: Texas 2005," n.d., <http:// www.usdoj.gov/dea/pubs/states/texas.html> (September 14, 2005).

Chapter 5. Ketamine

1. Personal interview with Paul Keefe, Norfolk County Juvenile Court, March 9, 2005.

2. Ibid.

3. *Drug Facilitated Sexual Assault Resource Guide*, National Drug Intelligence Center and George Mason University, Alexandria, Virginia, May 2003, p. 9.

4. Personal interview with Paul Keefe.

5. Ibid.

6. Ibid.

7. Ibid.

8. Ibid.

9. Ibid.

10. Ibid.

11. Ibid

12. Ibid.

13. C. Kuhn, et al., *Buzzed: The Straight Facts About the Most Used and Abused Drugs From Alcohol to Ecstasy*, 2d ed. (New York: W.W. Norton & Co., 2003), p. 86.
14. "Ketamine Timeline," n.d., <http://www.erowid.org/chemicals/ketamine/ketamine_timeline.php3> (November 13, 2004).
15. Ibid.
16. "DEA to Control 'Special K' for the First Time," July 13, 1999, <http://www.dea.gov/pubs/pressrel/pr071399.htm> (November 12, 2004).
17. "DEA Arrests 8 in International Ketamine Distribution Ring," October 2, 2002, <http://www.dea.gov/pubs/states/newsrel/mia100202.html> (January 13, 2005).
18. Ibid.
19. "Intelligence Bulletin: Ketamine," July 2004, <http://www.usdoj.gov/ndic/pubs10/10255/index.htm> (November 12, 2004).
20. "Ketamine Addiction," n.d., <http://www.Drug-rehabs.org/faqs/FAQ-ketamine.php> (December 2, 2004).
21. Kuhn, et al., p. 100.
22. Personal interview with Trinka Porrata, club-drug consultant and former narcotics detective, Los Angeles Police Department, September 9, 2005.
23. D. C. Javitt and J. T. Coyle, "Decoding

Schizophrenia," *Scientific American*, January 2004.

24. Kuhn, et al., p. 100.
25. Ibid., pp. 104, 251.
26. *Drug Facilitated Sexual Assault Resource Guide*, National Drug Intelligence Center and George Mason University, Alexandria, Virginia, May 2003, pp. 10–11.
27. Personal interview with Steve Cordes, San Diego Police Department, March 28, 2005.
28. Ibid.
29. Kuhn, et al., p. 105.
30. M. LeBeau and A. Mozayani, eds., *Drug-Facilitated Sexual Assault: A Forensic Handbook* (San Diego: Academic Press, 2001), p. 257.
31. "Drug Facts: Club Drugs," n.d., <http://www.whitehousedrugpolicy.gov/drugfact/club/index.html> (November 20, 2004).
32. Kuhn, et al., p. 107.
33. Personal interview with Dr. Alex Stalcup, medical director, New Lease Treatment Center, California, September 14, 2005.
34. "Other Dangerous Drugs," National Drug Threat Assessment 2004, April 2004, <http://www.usdoj.gov/ndic/pubs8/8731/odd.htm> (January 13, 2005).

Chapter 6. Treatment

1. Trinka Porrata, "GHB and Its Analogs: The Hidden Curse of Addiction," June 24, 2000,

<http://www.projectghb.org/addiction/rpt062400.htm> (February 7, 2005).

2. Ibid.
3. Ibid.
4. Ibid.
5. Ibid.
6. Ibid.
7. Ibid.
8. Ibid.
9. Ibid.
10. Ibid.
11. Personal interview with Trinka Porrata, club-drug consultant and former narcotics detective, Los Angeles Police Department, September 9, 2005.
12. Ibid.
13. Ibid.
14. Trinka Porrata, "GHB and Its Analogs: The Hidden Curse of Addiction."
15. C. Kuhn, et al., *Buzzed: The Straight Facts About the Most Used and Abused Drugs From Alcohol to Ecstasy*, 2d ed. (New York: W.W. Norton & Co., 2003), pp. 201–202.
16. Trinka Porrata, "GHB and Its Analogs: The Hidden Curse of Addiction."
17. Personal interview with Trinka Porrata.
18. Ibid.
19. "Rohypnol," n.d., <http://www.brown.edu/student_services/health_services/health_

education/atod/od_rohypnol.htm> (March 19, 2005.)

20. Personal interview with Dr. Alex Stalcup, medical director, New Lease Treatment Center, California, October 10–12, 2005.

21. Ibid.

22. Ibid.

23. Ibid.

24. Ibid.

25. Personal interview with Dr. Alex Stalcup.

26. "Ketamine," Spencer Recovery Centers, Inc., n.d., <http://www.ketamine-effects.com/> (March 7, 2005).

27. "Ketamine Addiction," n.d., <http://www.drug-rehabs.org/faqs/FAQ-ketamine.php> (February 7, 2005).

28. Personal interview with Dr. Alex Stalcup.

29. Ibid.

30. Ibid.

31. M. LeBeau and A. Mozayani, eds, *Drug-Facilitated Sexual Assault: A Forensic Handbook* (San Diego: Academic Press, 2001), p. 16.

32. Ibid., p. 2.

33. Personal interview with Dr. Alex Stalcup.

34. Ibid.

35. Ibid.

FURTHER READING

Books

Aronson, Virginia. *How To Say No.* Philadelphia, Penn.: Chelsea House, 2000.

Blachford, Stacey L. and Kristine Krapp, Eds. *Drugs and Controlled Substances: Information for Students.* Detroit, Mich.: Thomson/Gale, 2003.

Esherick, Joan. *Dying for Acceptance: A Teen's Guide to Drug- and Alcohol-Related Health Issues.* Philadelphia, Penn.: Mason Crest Publishers, 2005.

Graves, Bonnie. *Drug Use and Abuse.* Mankato, Minn.: LifeMatters, 2000.

Internet Addresses

ClubDrugs.gov
<http://www.clubdrugs.gov>
Read about the dangers of club drugs from this site from the National Institute on Drug Abuse (NIDA).

Teens: Stories, Info, & Help
<http://www.drugfree.org/Teen>
Learn more about predatory drugs and other drugs.

INDEX